From Misery to Happiness

Kawali
Publishing

Copyright © 2020 Shayne Neal

All rights reserved. No part of this book may be reproduced in any form or by an electronic or mechanical means, including information storage and retrieval systems, without permission in writing from the publisher, except by a reviewer who may quote brief passages in a review.

Quantity sales and special discounts are available to corporations, associations, and others. For details, contact the publisher below.

Book Design: Shayne Neal

Cover Design Assistance: "Does My Book Cover Suck" Facebook group

Cover Assistance: Design by Kat

Final Edits: Chantell Lima & Suzanne Zwezdaryk

First edition 2020

10 9 8 7 6 5 4 3 2 1

ISBN   978-0-9937440-2-0 (hardcover)
ISBN   978-0-9937440-0-6 (paperback)
ISBN   978-0-9937440-1-3 (digital book)

Kawali Publishing

www.KawaliPublishing.com

From Misery to Happiness

A poetic journey through love, loss, and second chances.

Shayne Neal

Dedication

I would like to dedicate this book to Stacey, the woman who found the courage to divorce me.

I don't think that Stacey has ever been a fan of poetry, and surely not mine in particular, but she was absolutely the driving force behind the publishing of this poetry book. Her grand, creative oversight has been a blessing in my life since before we were first married in 1991. She will undoubtedly continue to be a driving force in my publishing and writing adventure. There are no words for how much I appreciate Stacey for everything she does and who she is. She challenges me, she supports me, she loves me, and she accepts me (when she doesn't want to kill me).

I could ask for no more from a partner.

Table of Contents

Introduction 1
A Virtual Letter 4
Over You 8
Pals 10
As One 12
I Am Here 14
I Believe 16
Live Without 20
Fairy Tale 22
Captivate 24
Stranger 26
Sands of Society 28
Feeling Underdressed 32
Could I? 34
Young Love 36
The Bridge 38
Amanda 40
The Puzzle 42
Fear Not Fear 44
Storms 46
The Knight 48
Education 50
Tragic Loss 52
Muse 56
Lessons in Love 61
Special Thanks 66
Acknowledgements 67
Kickstarter Acknowledgement Section 67
Reading Suggestions 69
About the Author 71

Introduction

These poems are probably NOT what you are expecting. When I think of modern poetry, I think of this awesome quote…

"Poetry for people who don't like poems." (@itsdivya on YouTube)

WHAT MAKES THIS POETRY BOOK SPECIAL?

I want to take a moment to explain how much I have enjoyed writing poetry in my life. This first book has gone through so many changes that I barely recognize it. Each poem in the book is followed by a description of the inspiration or writing process that accompanied the verse. In some, the inspiration was a waitress that I was too shy to say hello to. In others, inspiration came from a homeless person, or a novel that I turned into a poem; and yet others were inspired by my ex-wife. We will be talking more about her later.

These descriptions are almost more like diary entries in that some of them really saw me bare my soul on paper. The descriptions are incredibly personal, and Stacey and I have had some unpleasant conversations about both the poems and descriptions. I have stood my ground on not changing much from the original wording, but I have given Stacey a veto on all the poems for this book. You will learn more than you probably want to about both of my marriages if you make it to the end… more than Stacey had planned I am sure.

Sometimes I tell who inspired the poem and who it is dedicated to and every poem has a lesson. These lessons may be something you already know, or they may be something that you disagree with; but I hope they will all give you something to think about.

CONCEPT

Many people have asked where the idea of writing a poetry book with descriptions came from and the idea was born from the online chat rooms of the 1990's. I was recovering from a back injury and looking for something to do with my 8 and 10 year old daughters and I just laid there for hours in bed watching them talk to people online. I met some amazing people in there, and one of the places I spent a lot of time at was the Poetry Café on the Excite network. These people often asked where a poem came from and it was in telling those stories that the idea for the book grew. I have written a description for every poem since then.

WARNING

My poetry is definitely not going to be for all poetry fans. While I would love it if you loved all of them, that is probably not very realistic. I would settle for just one of them connecting with you enough to have a positive impact on your life.

You might not like the idea of me telling you why I wrote the poem, or about the poem's inspiration, and if that's the case, I invite you to skip the descriptions completely. If you are really into modern poetry, the idea of rhyme might turn you off as well, and you might get more out of reading the descriptions and skipping the poems. I will admit that, for the most part, my poems are more Dr. Seuss than "Milk & Honey".

Keep in mind that any meaning or emotion you take from the poem, is infinitely more meaningful than my inspiration or intent. That is the nature of poetry to me.

THE COVER

Having my wife on the cover seems so natural to me, especially considering the title that we decided on. She was, after all, the cause of much of my misery and most of my happiness. The name, "From Misery to Happiness", came from conversations with Kickstarter supporters and my family after many of my suggestions were vetoed over and over again. I believe in serendipity and the final title so perfectly fits my poetic journey that nothing else could have felt this right.

RECOMMENDATION

If you read the description first, you might find that the poems read differently. It is a good idea to read the poem at least once before the description. Fill your imagination with the words and try to figure out if it means anything to you before trying to figure out what I meant (if anything). Sometimes you will hit the nail on the head. Sometimes you will think that I was hit in the head, and often, you will think that I need a mental health professional.

Hopefully my ADHD doesn't drive you more mad than necessary to enjoy the book.

My greatest recommendation is that you read some poetry. If you can't come to terms with my prose, go with some RH Sin or Randall McNair, but read something.

Books do nothing but raise monitors, but people who read books, change the world.

Shayne Neal

A Virtual Letter

Hello mom, hello dad, I'm writing just to say,
    That I found some friends I really love;
People I trust who talk and listen,
    True friends when push comes to shove.

When I flip through my little black book,
    It makes me happy and proud;
But when I tell these crazy friends,
    They just smile and **LOL**.

They are always there when I need help,
    And I am always here for them;
And if I ever think I am being a bother,
    They simply say **NP**.

I try to make them all smile and laugh,
    Sometimes I make them cough;
And if I ever need a boost,
    They can make me **LMAO**

Friendship is a serious gift,
    And one where I won't lack;
No matter how bad I have to pee,
    I always say **BRB**.

There are things I know you don't understand,
    Like why I mailed a letter from right next door.
I still love you both but the phone's always busy,
    Letting these friends make me **ROTF**.

A Virtual Letter

This is a tough description to write because what I wrote back in 1998 started out like this, "If you are familiar with all the chat rooms that are virtually everywhere on the Internet you will understand this poem and probably Laugh Out Loud."

Well it isn't 1998 anymore, and almost nobody knows what a chat room is today. We used to pick little pictures called avatars, that made us feel like different people. People rarely used pictures of themselves, but it did happen. Those little avatars would basically take turns typing in a room filled with 20 other people all talking at the same time. In the Poetry Café, people respectfully took turns talking. It was the beginning of Internet jargon for me and I wrote a poem about it. The host of the Café that night was called "aoife" and she loved poems about the chat room. I ran this one by her and she was quite pleased.

The problem today is not that no one knows the jargon. Everyone still uses the same acronyms today but in texting and social media. I laugh when I read the poem today because our kids have no idea what the correlation is between the internet and telephone. For those of you that still don't get it, back in the last millennia if you wanted to use the internet you basically used your phone line and your phone was effectively busy the entire time. You also have to remember that there were no cell phones. The phone line in the house went to a phone with buttons on it that was plugged into the wall. Yes, it had a cord and it was the only phone for everyone in the house to share.

Maybe just enjoy the parts of the poem that you do understand and just know that people online before 2000 had it much rougher than you did. You truly are living in the greatest time this planet has ever seen.

So now for the people who truly have no idea what I am talking about…

If you substitute the following words where you see the acronyms, it will make more sense and rhyme.

- LOL — Laugh Out Loud
- NP — No Problem
- LMAO — Laugh My Ass Off
- BRB — Be Right Back
- ROTF — Roll On The Floor

And that brings us to another problem. My wife thinks my poems all sound like Dr. Seuss books because I love rhyming couplets and quatrains so much. I have at least one poem in this book that is free verse but that was because someone once told me that I could only write with one type of stanza and I love a challenge.

The more accurate description is that I liked writing music and poetry in one style. And part of me struggles with poetry that doesn't have a rhyme structure. Think of old dogs and new tricks when you think of me.

DEDICATION: To all those who remember the chat rooms of the 90's and made the choice to disconnect their home phone for that world-wide-web thing.

LESSON: As much fun as you can have online, always value a real friendship over something virtual. Do yourself a favor and phone, text, or message someone you haven't seen in six months and ask if they are available for coffee or something. Challenge yourself to do this every month. Turn it into a habit and do it for the rest of your life.

Shayne Neal

Over You

I often stand outside at night
    And count the stars that grace the sky,
I see up there, a thief in the dark
    As he holds the twinkle from your eye,
The sun rises and the sky is blue,
And I am glad I'm over you,

The evening sees my lonely walks
    Through the woods not knowing where,
I find a glade of flowers and trees
    Where your scent still fills the air,
The morning brings an early dew,
And I am glad I'm over you,

I close my eyes on the darkened beach
    And hear the sounds of each wave roll,
Waking up here in the morning sun
    I feel your warmth comfort my soul,
I touch the water and know it's true,
That I'm so glad I'm over you,

Over You

In reality, I lived this poem's description. I actually fell asleep on a beach on Vancouver Island one night and woke up with the most comforting feeling that I was going to get back together with my ex-wife. I woke up and did a double-take because I thought she was there with me. I lay there in the sand and wrote the first draft of this poem... despite my apparent mental state.

I love the conflicting nature of how confident the words are about how "over" I was about someone and then clearly, I was NOT over that person. The implication in each stanza is that I stayed out all night thinking about a twinkle in someone's eye, their scent in a glade, or their warmth on a beach. Trust me, if you go for a long walk and think about someone until the sun rises, you are not over them. I wanted to make it humorous how confident a person can be about something they clearly were not correct about.

INSPIRATION: Stacey inspired this poem. She may have divorced me, but during our time apart I was quite convinced that I was the cause of all her pain. While I was not being very objective back then, I forced myself to deal with quite a bit of guilt. That led to many moments waking up on beaches and questioning my sanity.

DEDICATION: I would like to dedicate this to everyone who struggles to get over a lost love. It was a challenge for me, and although I believe I handled it quite well in the end, it was one of the most difficult things in my life. The challenges made me a stronger person, but probably a colder and more distant person. I am not sure that my ex-wife would think of that as an improvement, but now I handle stress and problems much better in my personal and professional life. While I enjoy being "that person", I am not sure it is always the healthiest aspect of my mental health.

You are going to see more than a few examples of how well I was dealing with getting over my first marriage even years after it ended. Much like this poem, I was not getting over it very well at all. In future poems we are going to be getting even more personal. If you are the type of person who says TMI a lot (Too Much Information), you might not feel very comfortable reading the rest of this book, and likely not any of my poetry books. Some of these descriptions might surprise you, even if we were old friends in my backyard, sitting around a fire.

LESSON: Be content with your choices. The human heart has no room for regret. But also, don't be afraid to not give up on love. Society tells us that it is okay to throw love away too easily. I think this makes for too many unhealthy old people.

Pals

Pals are the only things that last
    In a world that celebrates divorce;
Because pals are what good friends become
    When friendship takes its course.

Pals can sit and talk about things
    That others wouldn't dare;
They discuss love, past and present,
    And anything they choose to share.

Pals are friends who can disagree
    But when push comes to shove;
They join their hands with firm grips
    And show the strength of love.

Pals don't have to talk every day
    Sometimes they go quite a while;
But when they call, they always know
    They'll be greeted with a smile.

Pals are people who are always there
    When troubled times arrive;
Because being a pal, and having a pal
    Can make you feel alive.

Pals

What can I say about Pals except that it was inspired by my pals. In all stages of life, I have had men who have held a place in my heart. I don't talk to all of them anymore, but I would do anything for any one of them at the drop of a dime... or whatever pay phones cost nowadays... do we still have payphones?

If you have never had a pal or aren't sure what the difference is between a pal and a friend, go watch Young Guns. It is an old movie but it's a great one. Pals. You'll get it.

DEDICATION: I have many friends, but I want to dedicate this to my oldest pals... most of whom I haven't talked to since I broke my back, or earlier, but here are a few and the year we met:

Wayne G (1975), Michael L (1981), Curt C (1982), Craig M (1982), Dena P (1983), Mike M (1987), Ryan B (1992), Charles K (1997)

I was going to deliberately keep this just to guys, but I miss those long talks with Dena on the bus each day in high school. I loved that girl. She was a great pal. I have tried to track down some of these people but to no avail. My google-fu is just too weak. That might be a future project I need to find some time for.

I would be lucky if I talked to four of them in the past decade. That makes me sad, but it does not make them any less of a pal.

LESSON: Do what it takes to find an old pal or meet a new one. Nobody should live life without knowing someone they would give theirs for.

As One

Looking back on memories we share,
I see friendships truly rare,
      What more could we have done;
But witness a joining of life,
With you two as husband and wife,
      Knowing your minds now think as one.

Together you just seem right,
Like the morning and sunlight,
      Together you shine like the sun;
As we bring together two souls,
And this marriage unites your goals,
      Your lives will go on as one.

I am happy to say,
That I'll remember today,
      For all the joy and fun;
For all the people I've met,
And all the tears I've wept,
      As your hearts began beating as one.

As One

I knew a girl named Heather once. She lived in Calgary and was a nurse at one of my healthcare providers when I was in rehab learning how to walk again (the first time). I did a lot of rehab trying to get away from wheelchairs, walkers, and canes over the years. But rehab is for quitters, so no more about that.

Heather and I flirted a lot, but I never actually met her. She had an amazing voice though. That should have scared her. If we get around to talking about how Stacey and I met, you will truly understand.

At any rate, everything we did and said was all in fun. I was at a place in my life back then where nothing would have ever happened. I honestly thought there was still a 100% chance of remarrying my ex and I wouldn't have done anything to jeopardize that. But I sure liked talking to her every week.

One of our conversations ended up talking about my poetry and she asked if I could write a poem for her friend, Sheri, who had to read something at a wedding a few weeks later. I don't know if Sheri ever read the poem, but I wrote it for her anyway... and I sure loved writing it.

DEDICATION: To all my married friends. Stick with it! It is so worth it!

LESSON: Don't be one of those people who say they don't need someone to love. Seek love out! It should be the most important goal in your life aside from your relationship with a higher power, if you believe in one.

"Love has many pains, but celibacy has no pleasures." I am going to give credit here to Samuel Johnson even though I changed "marriage" to "love".

And that line about "rehab is for quitters" was on a t-shirt I wore to rehab more than once. I thought it was hilarious. The doctors and staff? Not so much.

I Am Here

You stood by me forever and a day,
    I could never explain quite why;
I never presumed to understand,
    I actually never tried.

I always seemed to take much more,
    Then I ever seemed to give;
You always tried to give me more,
    Then I ever needed to live.

As friendships go, I could not desire,
    Any more than I ever had;
You helped pull me through the dark,
    When things were pretty bad.

Now that I'm back on my feet,
    And my head's a little straight;
You can be sure if you need me,
    You will never have to wait.

I Am Here

Some of these poems are hard to talk about now. It is way more difficult than I thought it would be to reflect on things I wrote when I was pulled between loving my ex-wife too much to commit to another woman; and wishing that she would just marry another man so that I could find a way to move on.

These poems often have mixed feelings about the woman I love and about a woman I wanted to love. Here I am, over 20 years later, happily married to my ex-wife... wondering how the hell to explain what was going through my mind back then. How do I write about wanting to love another woman? Is it possible without hurting my wife? I sure hope so, because I honestly believe that there are words in here that can help someone. I do not ever recall writing an angry word about my ex-wife, but sad words flowed like rivers.

Remember way back when I told you that this book was going to get personal? I was writing this poem trying to come to grips with the crap that I had put my ex-wife through during our first marriage. It was no short list.

She was a good friend. I was a kid who didn't know what he wanted, had no idea how to get it, and was absolutely not prepared to do the work that was required to be a husband or father. I am still lazy, but now I am ambitiously lazy. I am willing to bust my butt today to relax tomorrow. I work harder and longer than most people I know because I see past the light at the end of the tunnel while others are focused on it.

I hope that all my family and friends know that I am here... I am here for them... anytime they need anything that I can provide.

DEDICATION: To Stacey, the woman I have loved since I first heard her voice in 1987. I will always be here for you.

LESSON: Love is not easy, but it is worth it.

I Believe

I believe that there is a purpose
    For each person's place in life,
Even though we don't understand
    How good can come from strife.

I believe that in the master plan
    Happiness comes somewhere, someway,
But when our troubles seem severe
    Nobody knows quite what to say.

I believe, like old Nietze,
    Our troubles might make us stronger,
But they also might give strength to others
    Who can't handle their lives much longer.

I believe these people might grow
    As they watch us struggle to cope,
They might finally see that life is worth living
    And through our living we might give them hope.

I Believe

This poem was written because a friend was personally touched by suicide. This friend made a comment that I would never be able to write something meaningful about the topic because I did not understand what he was going through. I do not believe that you have to live through something to understand it, especially if you are a phlegmatic personality. I am not, by the way. I am a choleric, which is the total opposite. But my personality loves a challenge more than anything and I jumped at this one.

He was partially correct though, in that empathy is not something that comes very naturally to my overbearing personality. What he never considered, was that I had been studying personalities for years and knew where my strengths and weaknesses were, and had been working on my empathy already, or lack thereof. I may be short on empathy, but I have more than enough compassion to make up for it.

Compounded with that, was that I consider myself crazy creative. I feel like I can write about anything and write well about it. Over-confidence is another enjoyable aspect of my personality.

For the record, I have since been very personally touched by suicide and I can tell you that those who say you can't understand without being touched by it are simply wrong. They are going through a lot and their judgement is likely clouded. Be nice to them and be understanding, but don't take what they say to heart. It might take some work, but you can absolutely understand what they are going through without going through it.

If I was wrong, then how would shrinks – I'm sorry - mental health professionals, help people unless they had gone through all the problems they treat? Do I have to remind you that I am NOT a mental health professional? I love the mental health industry but most of my personal experience comes from behind a bar or from the I.T. department of dozens of companies. I loved that people would tell bartenders their life stories after a few drinks. Afterall, everyone wants a pal. See what I did there? Apologies to Gerald Pauschmann, but I love that line and I bought the shirt, so I feel sanctioned to use it.

DEDICATION: To anyone suffering with a mental illness.

LESSON: ADHD is not a mental illness even though the government says it is. It is an amazing blessing if you learn how to use it and stop using it to play a victim.

Depression is significantly more serious, and everyone should be taught to recognize warning signs in school so that we are better prepared as a society, to help those who need us in the future.

Shayne Neal

Live Without

There are things that I want,
And things that I need,
And things I just can't live without.

The valleys and mountains,
The waterfalls and fountains,
The fresh morning dew and you.

The grass, the trees,
The rivers, and the seas,
A mountain lake view and you.

The sunsets, full moons,
Warm lakes, and lagoons,
A deep sky blue and you.

Singing birds, fresh air,
Dolphins, and the bear,
A stroll through the zoo with you.

There are things that I want,
And things that I need,
And things I just can't live without.

Butterflies, bright flowers,
Snowflakes, and spring showers,
A love strong and true and you.

Live Without

You are going to see a theme of me falling for waitresses. Most of them were physically gorgeous but more than a few had something not so tangible as a beautiful body, sensuous eyes, or an alluring voice. Kandal of course, had it all.

I would love to tell you that she had an amazing personality. I would love to tell you how funny she was and how much she comforted me, but I didn't actually build up the confidence to talk to her much. I brought flowers to her at work one day and she was totally overwhelmed by the act. I was overwhelmed by her over-reaction, like she had never received flowers before.

Kandal might have been the inspiration for this poem but I never actually asked her out, so I need to dig deep and think about other amazing women in my life that made me feel the way these words made me feel... make me feel.

The first stanza was the base of the poem where each of the three lines represented some belief pattern from my life. Each following stanza has three correlating lines for each of... a want... a need... and something I can't live without. I loved this poem for a card, but it was turned down by several companies including Blue Mountain Arts... who was by far my favorite for greeting card poetry.

This was one of my poems that finally saw print in some long-forgotten publication.

DEDICATION: The poem is dedicated to all those who have a desire or a need to have someone or something that they feel like they can't live without... and not just the guys that Kandal served lunch to in Nisku.

LESSON: Passion isn't everything, but everything is better with passion, especially if you have ADHD. I hope that you all find that passion about something or someone. Never stop looking for it. Once you find it, fight for it with every breath.

And guys, here is something I used to do when I wanted some romance in my life, without being able to get any romance. I would go to a mall and buy a couple dozen long stem roses with individual water picks on each. Then I would randomly hand a rose to women I passed walking around the mall or on the way back to my hotel. It always made me remember Kandal.

Fairy Tale

I wish you could somehow understand,

> *Some way I wish you could see,*

This man inside, who I am, this man I strive to be.

I keep him hidden so you won't laugh,

> *But he wants to make you smile,*

I yearn to open my heart to you, in a tender loving style.

I dream of a day when your hand is in mine,

> *And we sit alone and look eye to eye,*

I wish that dream didn't feel to me, so much like a lie.

If I allowed you to hold that man,

> *I know we would never let go,*

And happily-ever-after, we would come to know;

…And a fairy tale would be born.

Fairy Tale

I wrote this when I was struggling with my divorce (do you see a theme here?). It was a very long three years. During that time, I met some women that made me believe that I could have a new life someday and start over, but I simply refused to believe that my marriage could not be saved. It was harder to hold that faith after I received the papers saying that my divorce was finalized, but I held on... often beyond reason.

This poem held two very hard meanings to me. On one hand, I really believed that I could be a better man for my ex-wife. I believed in my heart that we could have a great marriage. While I was believing that though, my ex-wife wasn't talking to me. I did not hear her voice for 14 months at one point. It was very hard to hold that faith.

At the same time, I believed that I could become the man that one particular woman deserved. She was a wonderful woman with an amazing baby. While I wanted to be the best example of what a man could be for her, I was still hung up on my ex-wife, and in turn, being a horrible example of a man.

How could I be with one woman physically and want another woman emotionally? How could I commit my heart to a woman that I thought I could love, no matter how amazing she was, if my heart still belonged to another woman? I could not, so I did not, and it almost killed me.

This was absolutely one of the most difficult things I ever struggled with. I thought loving a woman who didn't love you was the hardest thing to live with, but it was harder to love two women at once.

I have never regretted a moment of my struggles, and I never regretted convincing Leta to convince her daughter to hand her baby to a stranger on a ferry. Thank you Leta. I suppose I have to tell that story in another book too.

DEDICATION: To Tina. I cannot tell you how much it ripped me apart not being able to give my heart to her like she deserved. I wasn't fair to her. She deserved better and I honestly thought there was a way that I could be that man... that I could have that fairy tale... and be a part of that fairy tale forever with her.

LESSON: Follow your heart.

As much as I would have loved to have given my life to Tina, and as much as she was wonderful and deserving of better than me; by following my heart and waiting for my ex-wife, I have been blessed by the most wonderful life I could have ever imagined.

Captivate

I don't understand how I can miss,
    Someone who doesn't know I exist;
        Yet each night, safe with my dreams,
We are friends that have not kissed.

I stand by and wait for a chance,
    To squeeze in some subtle "Hi's";
        But my body can't talk, and my heart is lost,
As you captivate my eyes.

I wish you could dream, like I have been,
    And somehow awake without end;
        In hopes that you could suddenly see,
How I wish to be your friend.

As I watch you, I know I should talk,
    And my silence takes its toll;
        As every little thing you do,
Captivates my soul.

Captivate

This was inspired, like many, by a waitress. I did a lot of eating out alone back in those days. Kassidy and I never really talked outside of my quiet dinners by myself. I probably drank a lot more than I needed to when she was working but every refill was another opportunity to say "Hi" to her. Lost opportunities.

For the record as well, I was drinking some kind of soft drink at the Boston Pizza in Edmonton, not getting drunk.

This poem makes me want to talk about how Stacey and I met. There is no doubt that this is a great story, and as fun as it is to share with friends in the back yard, it might cause another divorce (or murder).

Way back in my youth, when I was 17 and only a few months out of high school, I first heard Stacey's voice on the phone. I will save the whole story for another day, or another book, but you need to understand that over the next four months, I fell in love, told Stacey that I wanted to have a dozen kids with her, promised her the whole world, and proposed to her. After all that, she still decided to meet me.

I get captivated very easily it seems, and I am a real sucker for a soothing voice.

Stacey used to sing to me over the phone while we both lay in bed in different cities. What a wonderful way to fall asleep. I can tell you stories about that too, but they won't make me look very good and we have enough of that already.

DEDICATION: While Kassidy may have been the inspiration, I need to dedicate this poem to Kandie from Omaha, Nebraska. She exemplified purity and innocence and I cherished my time with her. I never did meet her IRL (In Real Life), but we talked on the phone and spent many hours online together. She once told me that she read this poem every morning because it meant so much to her.

I wish that everyone could be captivated by the kind of love that I have felt since 1987, since the first time I heard Stacey's voice.

LESSON: Finding someone who captivates you like this will help you to open up so you can captivate others. Do not link this solely to physical beauty. It might just as easily be someone's laugh, their confidence, or a voice on the telephone.

Stranger

Someday you may meet a stranger,
    Who can be a dear friend too;
        One who at first meant little,
            If anything at all to you.

But then maybe just a little grin,
    Or maybe a wink of an eye;
        Is all it takes to open your heart,
            To make you suddenly say "Hi".

That one little word might start,
    Something great and grand;
        Cause you never know if the future,
            Will see you needing a hand.

That hand might come from a friend,
    Whom you once called a stranger;
        So try to risk a broken heart,
            With just a little bit of danger.

Stranger

"The Stranger" was written in Calgary, Alberta, and inspired by a little girl named Morgan who kept walking up to my sister and I as we sat on the edge of a wading pool. She was incredibly shy but each time that she passed I would smile, wave, or wink at her and she slowly became less defensive.

Half an hour later she was sitting on the edge with us explaining how she wasn't allowed to talk to strangers. The whole time she was sharing her animal crackers with me. Once she swam up to us and explained that she was a baby whale.

"Do you like baby whales", she asked?

"Well, I have never met a baby whale before today", I replied, "so you are for sure my favorite baby whale".

She was quite pleased by this. Her mother and aunt came to steal her away as the sun set and I went home with a priceless memory.

DEDICATION: To Morgan... still my favorite baby whale.

LESSON: Keep your heart open and always encourage creative imagination in kids. They will likely grow up soon enough and become mindless drones. Do not be a catalyst to this loss of innocence.

Sands of Society

Blood had been bled, the body's skin had been shed,
    In the desert and all its heat.
The grief of the world, all the labor you toiled,
    Had run you down in the street.

I found you and caressed, because you were so stressed,
    Slowly dying in this windy wasteland.
You took my embrace, I wiped sand from your face,
    As is expected of me as a man.

I gave moisture to your lips, as you fell into my grips,
    You were simply too tired to walk.
The world made you low, but chivalry had to show,
    Without requiring you to talk.

I'll help you from the sand, from your pain so grand,
    This is how I wanted my love shown.
For each blister and bruise, it meant more to not lose,
    In my fight to prove you weren't alone.

My goal was to save you from this world,
    Like I saved you from the sun;
But a few drops of water simply can't fix,
    The damage the world has done.

So, I'll give you my love and my life,
    And we'll see where everything goes;
I want your future world to be filled,
    With highs and not just lows.

Sands of Society

I was sitting at a public fountain writing because I love the relaxing sound of running water. On this particular day, in front of the city hall in Edmonton, there was a photo-shoot taking place and I was talking with Tracy, the photographer. Tracy talked to Blue and Stacey about my poetry book because the initial submission to publishers had a photo included for each poem as well. She mailed me a couple photos a month later and I was super impressed. Of course, now that I have not included photos in the book, her efforts have not resulted in much. It has been over 20 years since the photo was taken, so I don't think anyone will notice.

This poem symbolized what it meant to me to be a man in this world. I wish that I lived in a world where women were all happy being equal to men, and men were happy serving women. I want my daughters to be independent and self-sufficient, but I also want them to be able to be stay-at-home mothers if this life allows it and they want it. I believe that raising children is the most significant role anyone can perform in our world. I cannot think of anything that rivals its importance.

I want my daughters to be able to take care of themselves but to also know that it's okay to let someone take care of them. And they always need to know that I am here for them forever.

I only have three measures of success in this world. Did I guide, protect, and provide for my wife and children? I work very hard at this, but this world is a very hard place. I have been beaten down more than once and I know that my kids will feel pain and suffering as well.

I worry about those who are beat down in this world without any support system. I weep for their situation and love those who help and protect them.

DEDICATION: To Blue and Stacey and anyone who feels beaten by this world. Recent times have put us through life-changing turmoil, but we are a species of survivors... and to Heather. She knows why.

LESSON: There is always a silver lining. Find it.

This poem had a deeper and more symbolic meaning as well but with the vast number of atheists in the world, I thought I would try the politically correct thing and not even mention it.

Apparently, I am not a fan of political correctness.

Shayne Neal

Feeling Underdressed

It turns out I wasn't prepared for this.
The simple pressures that come with life.
The little things that make some frown,
In me, cause major strife.
    But now I see the cold cruel world.
    I'm too young to be this stressed.
    I stand out here alone at times,
    And I feel so underdressed.

Sometimes the world seems so dark.
My life doesn't have enough fun.
Sometimes I dream ahead to a future,
To a day when I can rest in the sun.
    I may have made bad choices in life,
    I might have failed life's basic test.
    Maybe that is why I feel alone,
    And why I feel so underdressed.

I haven't the courage to think of much else,
Then the life most people are used to.
I too can dream and wish on a star,
And pray that these things come true.
    Is there really hope for someone like me,
    Is there a chance that I'll ever be blessed?
    How could I pull myself out of this rut,
    So that my kids never feel underdressed?

Feeling Underdressed

This poem was inspired by a little three-year-old in Calgary's Eau Claire wading pool. He wanted to get in the water and he just dropped his clothes and jumped in. It was absolutely priceless. His name was Daniel and he was adorable.

I wrote the title to the poem at the top of a page in my notebook but had no idea what I was writing about it. I was staying in a hotel all weekend and just wandered around downtown looking for inspiration. I was actually working on a novel at the time but, since seeing Daniel in the afternoon, that title kept popping up.

Later that night, on my way back from a movie, I saw a young lady working in front of a skyscraper at what is often referred to as "the oldest profession in the world". Truly that girl was underdressed. The words started coming to me and after the woman moved on, she was replaced by a homeless guy taking a nap. I sat there on a park bench and let the world inspire my pen.

Every stanza has a part of the homeless, a part of the working girl, a part of little Daniel, and a part of me. There is a good chance there is a part of you in it if you ever felt trapped or forced into a situation that you never wanted in your life.

For Stacey, I prayed that she could hold it together and be the amazing mother that I knew she could be, and never feel like she let our children down. Millions of women are thrust into single-motherhood and none of them should ever feel underdressed.

I also think this sounds like something Stacey would have written. She may object and she would know how she feels much more than I would, but the point is that I "think" that this is how she feels.

Stacey stresses about everything. She worries way more about her children than she ever did about either of us. She spends so much energy thinking about what might be, often at the cost of what is. Hopefully my opposing personality provided some balance because I think stress is very hard on the soul.

INSPIRED by Daniel and the world that raised him.

DEDICATION: To society and its willing servants and slaves.

LESSON: May we find a way to give fresh starts to those who need them before we lose our opportunity, and our chance to be the best of what makes us human.

Could I?

You want me to stop loving you
Like you stopped loving me,
But there are some things that I can't do
And I wish that you could see.

Could I suppress the rising sun
Or keep the rain from falling down?
Could I just as easily live underwater
And hold my breath and never drown?

Could I keep grass from growing long
Or the trees from rising tall?
Could I make summer turn to spring
Without any winter at all?

Could I somehow, forget true love,
And risk never wearing another smile?
Could I throw away every memory
That has made my life worthwhile?

You want me to stop loving you
Like you stopped loving me,
But there are things I just can't do
And some things that just can't be.

Could I?

This poem is probably exactly what you thought it was after your first read. This was basically the story of my life. Stacey and I were divorced, and she asked me on several occasions to forget about her and move on. I had more than one opportunity and one that I actually wanted to take, but some things just can't be.

Stacey became pregnant after our divorce and everyone thought this would have made it easier for me to walk away, but it did not. It might have made the choice more difficult. She begged me to forget her and at one point I remember saying that "till death do us part" meant one of us needed to die so she could just relax and wait for a while. It really pissed her off and sadly, that might have made it more worthwhile back then. I would love to say that I used to be quite an ass but by using past tense, I might feel a little dishonest.

One day after our divorce, Stacey and I were driving, and she told me that she was pregnant and that she was no longer seeing her boyfriend. I think she told me in hopes that it would help me move on. I explained that it made zero difference to me. She made some comment about how we could never be together again because I could never raise another man's child. I asked her why she thought I would love my children more than his and she responded very matter-of-factly, because they came from me. I told her that I never loved any of our kids because they came from me, I loved them because they came from her... so how was this child going to be any different?

The fact that I am not the biological father of a child has never had any bearing on how I raised a child or how I felt. I do know though, that others do not share my feelings and are not as comfortable with me sharing such personal details in a book. They need to get over it.

They can write their own book and not share whatever they feel fitting.

My family will clearly never let me be a guest on Ellen.

DEDICATION: To Stacey, the most worthwhile wait in the world.

LESSON: Anything worth having is worth working for and waiting for.

Young Love

You lay beside me late at night,
But your eyes are a mile away.
    You try to explain your desires to me,
    But I don't understand a thing you say.

Sometimes you stare into distant space,
And I wonder where you are.
    I often wish I could live life like you,
    Just like a shooting star.

You love to create more work for others,
Extending a trying day.
    It seems you live without rhyme or reason,
    You live to eat, and sleep, and play.

But I still love you like you deserve,
Your presence has opened closed doors.
    And you bring a joy into my life,
    That I could never measure before.

Young Love

When I was living with Peggy and Thor for a year, their baby, Andrew, woke up one night at 4am. Since I was still up writing on the computer, I just got him a bottle and put him back to sleep in the living room. While we were laying on the sofa, he just stared out the window. Andrew was definitely the inspiration for the prose but as I often do, I twisted the meaning hours later as I composed line after line.

If you have ever loved someone who was so different from you, that you often couldn't understand what they were doing or why they were doing it, then you would understand a lot of the turmoil in the life that Stacey and I shared.

Almost every line of this poem was written as an apology to Stacey for the way I made her feel. My eyes are often wandering in another world and Stacey really likes to be in the present. I am often horrible with words and communicating, even for a writer, and she just wants me to read her mind. I live life like a shooting star, and she is steady like the setting sun... always predictable, planned, and prepared.

We aren't going to touch the second half of the poem because it starts with Stacey picking up my socks and just gets more embarrassing from there.

INSPIRED by Andrew.

DEDICATION: To Stacey for learning how to deal with my opposing personality. We are truly opposites that attract. I cannot imagine any two people who could disagree more fervently and think about killing one another one minute, and then be willing to die for one another the next minute.

LESSON: Take a personality test (or two) because this will give you huge insights into who you are and why you do the things you do. Live your life without thinking you have to change who you are to please someone else... and find someone who will put up with your faults because you make it worth the effort for them.

Don't forget to make it worth the effort.

The Bridge

The world seems to move around you,
    In weird and wonderful ways,
        With people in boats and cars and trains.
Yet evil and unhappiness everywhere,
    Cause others to sometimes fall,
        Your sanity somehow remains.

Strong is the base which holds me high,
    I am warm but I still shiver,
        You are the bridge over my river.

You are always there when others need,
    Especially for me,
        You stand to relieve our pain.
People keep putting pressure on you,
    Never questioning how you stand,
        Through the storms of wind and rain.

You allow some troubles to flow right by,
    As the taker and the giver,
        You are the bridge over my river.

The Bridge

This is a wonderfully dark poem about a bridge and at first read it seems that the bridge just takes a person back and forth across the river but it actually got a guy thinking hard about his life, when he was considering suicide and he decided that if the bridge could stand through all the turmoil then he could make it too.

The turmoil of the bridge is not storms of nature but of society because so many people don't come to the same decision and many commit suicide from the bridge. Sometimes the bridge is the taker of life and sometimes it is the giver.

In my hometown some citizens actually called for the closure of a bridge because so many people jumped from it.

We, as a society, need to spend less time talking about closing bridges, and less money on guardrails and chain link fences. We need to resolve the situations that put people on bridges with thoughts of ending their lives in the first place.

DEDICATION: To anyone struggling with depression... you are loved.

LESSON: Suicide is a dark and horrible thought that has hit very close to my life, but if we don't talk about it, we learn nothing; and if we learn nothing, then the greatest loss in suicide is to the living.

Amanda

I love to smell the flowers,
  And I love to taste the rain,
But when you're not beside me, I only feel the pain.

Do not delay in what you do,
  Waste no time returning to me,
I am filled with undying love, that I need you to see.

I lay awake alone at night,
  Living out my deepest fear,
The only thing I can recall, is desire to hold you near.

I pray for us to be together,
  Not apart like we are now,
I dream the morning light, brings you here somehow.

Amanda

I met Amanda on a flight to Vancouver in September of 1998. She was flying home from Edmonton after visiting her boyfriend who had moved to Alberta for a better job.

I could not help but think about how many times Stacey felt this way about me when I was working far from home. The flight could have lasted hours more, and I would have been content just listening to Amanda talk about Kolby. It was like peeking into the personal memories of my ex-wife and our life.

Considering that this was over 20 years ago, and the odds of our current society would be against it, I hope that Amanda and Kolby are both happy... and hopefully together.

DEDICATION: To everyone who struggles with long distance love.

LESSON: As hard as it is to say, the only lesson I have is to avoid long distance romance if possible. Find a better job at home or move your family. Long distance love can work but the effort is immense, as is the risk.

This is coming from a man who has done it more than once and will do it again in the future. It is a part of the life I chose.

The Puzzle

Our sorrow runs deep as we take the time,
    To acknowledge loneliness and grief;
Our loss may bring anger and confusion,
    We may seek to blame God as a thief.

We may wonder how to continue,
    To keep building the puzzle of life;
Now that a piece has been taken,
    Bringing nothing but turmoil and strife.

Each puzzle piece lays on a mat of tears,
    And even though one is now gone;
The puzzle of life continues each day,
    Each dusk is still followed by dawn.

How the pieces will continue to fit,
    You can seek help to understand;
Instead of placing blame on God,
    Pray for Him to lend you a hand.

Completing your puzzle of life,
    May be hard without someone you love;
But they are now waiting for you,
    Trying to build their puzzle above.

The Puzzle

The puzzle was a very personal gift to a good friend who lost her father. God played no small part in this one because I had no idea where to start. I sat down with the intent of staying up all night writing but within the first hour inspiration struck. At the time, I had never been to a funeral. I have since been to a few funerals for family members who all went to build new puzzles in the past few years.

I am not sure if it's because I am a cold-hearted ass or what, but I simply don't get affected at funerals like most people. Keep in mind that I am mostly comparing myself to Stacey and she is typically a bumbling mess at a funeral. She was affected so much by her mother's passing that I thought we were going to need to find professional help for our family.

This was hard on me because I live my life with only three goals; to guide, protect, and provide for my wife and children. After Stacey's mother passed away there was a period over a year-long where there was literally nothing I could do to make Stacey happy. It was very frustrating to have my controlling personality and not be able to help in any way. I was clearly not in control of anything.

DEDICATION: To those who have experienced loss and struggled to keep working on their puzzles.

LESSON: Use empathy and compassion accordingly. People dealing with loss of a loved one may need your support. Probably not me, but most other people. I say probably because I cannot imagine losing my wife or any of my kids. I might need your support after all.

Fear Not Fear

Why does fear exist?
Does it not breed hesitation in the soul of our desires?

We fear drowning when swimming deep,
We fear stumbling when running fast,
We fear falling when climbing high,
> And I recall fear of rejection preventing me from saying hello to you for way too long.

> But then I thought…

Fear holds my breath longer, allowing me to reach the surface,
Fear pushes my legs faster, so I can lunge across the finish,
Fear holds my grip stronger, letting me pull myself to the top,
> And I remember fear of losing you helped me to learn to be the person that you deserve.

> Fear gave me the greatest gift in the world… you.

I will fear not fear.

Fear Not Fear

This poem was inspired by a woman at a pool reading a book called "The Gift of Fear" (by Gavin de Becker) while her children were swimming. It got me thinking about the way that fear could benefit a person and I immediately thought of relationships. I was a brooding mess at the beginning of my divorce, and I let the fear of hurting another woman force me into a life of solitude.

My friends at the time were few and far between because I didn't want to get close to anyone. I used to think about how much I was missing out on because of my fear but just seeing her reading that book made me reassess my life.

I decided that day that I would wait for a woman beautiful enough to help me overcome my fears. I used my fears to make me a better man... a more patient man.

This poem marks my first foray into free verse. Do not get used to it. Because of my love of songwriting, I have this affinity for rhyme and rhythm. And I do not do haiku or limericks either.

As a young person, you might be able to fall in love with modern poetry. I don't want to criticize anyone's writing, but I simply don't understand how a few words can be a poem. Sometimes a word written backwards is a poem. Sometimes it is just a typo. Maybe I am too long winded to ever understand. You are welcome to let me know that you think I am wrong.

I am clearly not the magician that can write a few words and have you contemplating life for the afternoon. I wrote a poem once that had one line...

> I am not R. H. Sin.

But then who else is? I don't even dream of R. H. Sin perusing my poetry, but I would love if Steph Waloon would someday. How she would fit it into her reading schedule would be simply beyond my comprehension though.

DEDICATION: To men and women who let fear cripple them... or even affect them at all.

LESSON: How we overcome our fears helps us to learn and grow so we can better handle future fears. These lessons reinforce the idea that fear can be a positive quality.

Storms

I run headlong into the storm
    And never worry about the rain,
        The challenges and the risks
            Are always worth the pain.

Being there is half the fun
    Feeling the wind as it blows,
        But you never wanted or deserved
            Such erratic highs and lows.

The wind and rain, the hail and snow,
    Slow most people as they walk,
        But I am odd and seem to thrive
            On proving I'm a rock.

If you stand by me through these storms
    That I find myself in now,
        I aim to learn how to relax
            And enjoy our life somehow.

Storms

I have done a lot of editing of these descriptions for this book because some were written decades ago, and for most of them, I was still divorced. For this one, I talk about my daughter that my wife had while we were apart. When I wrote this, I had only seen her in the hospital the day after she was born but Stacey and I were not on speaking terms. I am including this description just as it was written 22 years ago...

This poem reflects how I used to live my life. I felt that I did my best work when I was stressed or under pressure and I may have been right, but now I am faced with the question, "was my best work worth losing my family?".

This was one of my poems inspired by Divine inspiration (that will piss off my mother). Out of the blue, for no reason, one line popped into my head... "I walked headlong into the storm". Two days later I saw it in my notebook and started playing with the rhymes and rhythm. The first verse flowed nicely and every time I read it, I wished that I had been man enough when I was married, to feel, act, and communicate these words to Stacey.

I believe that everything happens for a reason. Had I not gone through my trials with losing my family, this poem would never have been written (most wouldn't have been) and Casandra would never have been born. Therefore, I will dedicate "My Storms" to that special little girl who will always have a place in my heart and my life, even if she never knows it.

INSPIRED by God.

DEDICATION: Casandra and all my kids and siblings who have had to put up with my running headlong into storms, and to Stacey for being strong enough to walk away before my storms took too big a toll on her.

LESSON: Know your flaws and respect the people who put up with them... especially when thinking of their flaws. Invest time thinking of how your strengths can help you overcome the flaws in others before they bring out flaws in your personality.

For the record, 24 years later, I still love storms and spend way too much time in them to be healthy.

The Knight

I have grown into a mature woman indeed,
But it seems my life never fails;
    To attract only losers of the opposite sex,
    The worst of our species of males.
Where is the knight that was promised to me,
    In childhood fairy tales?

I wanted a man who is just like my dad,
Who was raised to have some respect;
    One I can trust to protect my heart,
    Without having to pass a test;
A guy who loves children and seniors as well,
    And helps damsels in distress.

Compared to my father it seems just a fact,
That every man somehow pales.
    I just want a man who would die for love,
    Who knows of men and males.
So where is the knight that was promised to me,
    In childhood fairy tales?

The Knight

One night I was wondering what caused women who had so much going for them to end up with such horrible examples of men. I wrote this poem while a woman I was dating was sleeping in the next room. Her name was Tina (it still is), and she was a very beautiful woman (probably still is). She was not just good looking, but she had an amazing voice and I am a sucker for a woman with an amazing voice.

She also had my emotional kryptonite, a baby. Tina was amazing and I instantly fell in love with her daughter, Ryanne. I struggled hard with this relationship and I could write another book about it... but this is about a poem inspired by Ryanne.

You could say that my ex-wife at the time had bad luck with men, but it was more because she was too picky. I didn't think I was that bad. Tina basically followed her boyfriend 3000 km from the Atlantic to the Pacific and as soon as he found out she was pregnant, he walked out of her life.

While I pined away for my ex-wife and my children, I prayed for a way to improve the lives of these two ladies. I wish that I knew a way to protect Ryanne, and all little girls, from men like Tina's ex. The only way I know to help them is to be a positive role model for young boys and men so that they understand what a real man is, and to teach young ladies to never settle for anything less.

DEDICATION: To Tina and Ryanne. Two girls who changed my life when it really needed a change. Also, to Chelsey, Chantell, Casandra, and Cydnee: four of the most important girls in the world to me. Without trying to make myself a suspect of a future crime, God help the man that hurts one of my daughters.

LESSON: More of an instruction, but if you have some free time, donate it to a youth organization so that you can be an example of a great role model. If you do not have the free time, make it. If you are not a great role model, find one to learn from. Our future generations need you very much. We need to teach our children to want more and to expect more, of themselves, and others. Men need to know there is more to being a man, than just being a male, and women need to know that they do not have to accept anything less than the knight of their dreams.

Education

A hundred years ago, there was a point you know,
   When educating fell on husband and wife.
Decades have come and passed, nothing it seems can last,
   Education succumbs to the circle of life.

Our families soon did grow, and parents had lives to sow,
   And each booming town sent their children to class.
As each schoolhouse reared, going back was never feared,
   And decisions were never questioned by the mass.

So, as our nation grew, schoolhouses became few,
   And we herded our kids into buildings of size.
Progress appeared to advance, never giving our people a chance,
   To foresee the fall of education's big rise.

Now that we've grown some more, the family again is our core,
   And we see our nation's educational strife.
Parents again take the roles, of teachers of minds and souls,
   And education succumbs to the circle of life.

Education

I have a knack for not agreeing with many public educators. I have met a few who I get along with very well but most of them home school their children. I have been moderately vocal with my disdain for where public education has gone, and that gets confused with any ill-feelings toward educators. Do not confuse the two. I love those who are willing to teach. I feel contempt for some of the things they teach and some of their methods, and much of this is out of their control.

Stacey has my utmost respect for being willing to take on the workload and responsibility for home schooling our children for the past 20 years. For many years I had lingering questions about our methods and reasons, but after two decades I only have four children left at home, and of the five that have escaped, a couple are married, one is engaged, and I even have some grandchildren on the way.

They are all happy and productive members of society and all are wonderful people, mostly due to the influence of their mother. I have some of the most well-rounded and intelligent kids I could hope for. I am so proud of each, and every one of them, and of my amazing wife for her incredible efforts in helping them get to where they are.

DEDICATION: To Stacey and all those amazing parents who invest their time enriching the lives of their children so they can learn what a bully is from TV shows and YouTube instead of from an actual bully.

LESSON: There is no such thing as quality time without quantity time. The idea that you could spend one hour a night with your children and have the same effect on them as a stay at home parent spending 12-16 hours a day with them is pure nonsense.

The same logic works for your marriage.

Tragic Loss

I knew a woman once, that lived with icy guilt,

Her conscience feared the dark, due to the life she built.

She cheated on a man, one that knew her through,

And though he loved her soul, her love was less than true.

She knew what she had done, she chose to live a lie,

In time it burned two souls, as truth met naked eye.

The night that lit a blaze, the guilt that owned her soul,

Set truthful things in motion, that God has seen unfold.

Through fiery rage he lifted her, above his head so high,

His lungs inhaled the flame, quite sure that one would die.

With one last painful breath, he threw her clear of harm,

Above his passion burned, with all his handsome charm.

With no love or lover, there lay a broken girl,
    Who lost nothing she loved,
        And lost her whole damn world.

Tragic Loss

This is a crazy poem because it started out as a short story, something I have always longed to write. That story was turning into a novel and as I wrote out the outline to see if there was any way that my writing ability could shorten it to a story, a poem emerged.

The thought of taking an 80,000 word novel and turning it into a 5000-word short story, seemed daunting at best, but somehow, I turned it into a wee little 150-word poem. I wish I understood how and why my brain did the things that it did. Somehow, I wrote a tragedy that I believe that Shakespeare would appreciate, and I fit it on a single page.

The book, and poem now, tells the story of a young woman's struggle as she fell in love with another man and lived a lie with her husband, even though he loved her with every fiber in his body. She didn't have the heart to leave him because she knew it would crush him forever.

She knew he would be devastated if she ever left him and she loved him too much to break his heart. She could also no longer live with the guilt of cheating on him. She somehow convinced herself that the only way out was to murder her husband. She may have had mental health issues but now you understand why I was having such a hard time with the short story concept. She set fire to their bedroom while he was sleeping and when he awoke to see her standing on the other side of the flames, he was confused... she told him that she was seeing another man and that she was so sorry that it had to end this way. She was instantly regretting her choices in life, but everything was burning around her, and she saw no way out.

As she was about to leave because she saw no way for her husband to survive, the ceiling crashed down on top of her. At that very instant, her husband jumped through the fire, pulled her from the floor and ran to throw her out a second-floor window to save her life.

She looked back up at him and realized that after everything she did to him, he still gave his life to save hers. She finally knew what true love was and she fell in love with her husband all over again... just in time to watch him burn alive in the world she started on fire. She now lay there, broken on the grass, watching everything important in her life burn to the ground.

DEDICATED: To those unlucky souls who believe in their heart that the whole world is against them.

LESSON: If you are making bad life choices, you probably should not try to resolve those situations with more bad life choices. I am not a huge fan of seeking help from mental health professionals because I am as stubborn as they come, but I am a strong advocate of help for those who need it (many mental health professionals are already making notes to look me up later).

If you keep finding yourself in a deeper hole, no matter what you try to do to improve your life, you need to do two things. First, stop digging. Clearly the same level of thinking that put you in the hole cannot help you escape. Secondly, seek out help from a friend who has what you want, a mentor with a vested interest in your future, or a professional who understands what you are going through.

Shayne Neal

Muse

You write what you know

So misery was my muse

Now I write of love

Muse

My son was nagging me because my poems all rhyme, he probably got that from his mother. He asked how I thought I could publish a poetry book without a haiku and I laughed at him. I have stated many times that I just don't write haiku and I certainly wasn't going to include one in my poetry book.

That is simply no longer true.

One of my fears of publishing a poetry book was always the fear of success or happiness. After getting my family back, I was worried that I would lose my edge. If I believed that my misery was my muse, would I be able to write anymore once I was happy?

It is a little messed up that I honestly believed that my ability to write poetry came from my misery; that the pain I was dealing with was giving me a superpower or something. I did prove to myself that I could still write after I was remarried. That was very comforting to me way back then and I continued writing novels and poems as a type of personal therapy. I find writing to be one of the most relaxing things in my world

I wrote this poem in 2020. I am now convinced that I did not love poetry, or excel at it, just because I was a broken man. I was wrong. Do not get used to that. Not me being wrong (I am wrong all the time). Don't get used to me *admitting* it though (due to a personality flaw that I haven't cared about enough to resolve).

INSPIRED by Ryan. My oldest son.

DEDICATED: To anyone who has self-doubt about their creative abilities.

LESSON: Believe in yourself.

You don't need me or some actor, musician, or anyone else to convince you. It starts with you *choosing* to believe that you can do anything you want… even write a haiku.

From Misery to Happiness

Thank you for reading my book,

I hope it was worth the look,

And if it won't take too long,

I'd love you to review it on Amazon

Because if you have no regrets about what you bought,

Maybe others would appreciate you sharing a thought.

Amazon reviews are extremely helpful for authors, thank you for taking the time to support me and my work.

Don't forget to share your review on social media and encourage others to read the collection as well.

Lessons in Love

This was actually one of the vetoed book titles and, for a while, the lessons were a major focus of the poetry book. There was some slight detouring and the lessons took a backseat on the cover as well as in the body of the book.

Heather Howe was one of our ARC readers (Advance Reader Copies) and in her suggestions, she thought it would be nice to see all the "lessons" combined at the end of the book. Let this be a lesson to you that you should sign up at our website to be an ARC reader for future books (www.KawaliPublishing.com).

Not only was Heather's opinion considered, but she helped bring the lessons back to life for me. Sometimes I don't see the forest for the trees. Thank you, Heather.

A Virtual Letter: As much fun as you can have online, always value a real friendship over something virtual. Do yourself a favor and phone, text, or message someone you haven't seen in six months and ask if they are available for coffee or something. Challenge yourself to do this every month. Turn it into a habit and do it for the rest of your life.

Over You: Be content with your choices. The human heart has no room for regret. But also, don't be afraid to not give up on love. Society tells us that it is okay to throw love away too easily. I think this makes for too many unhealthy old people.

Pals: Do what it takes to find an old pal or meet a new one. Nobody should live life without knowing someone they would give theirs for.

As One: Don't be one of those people who say they don't need someone to love. Seek love out! It should be the most important goal in your life aside from your relationship with a higher power, if you believe in one. "Love has many pains, but celibacy has no pleasures." I am going to give credit here to Samuel Johnson even though I changed "marriage" to "love".

I Am Here: Love is not easy, but it is worth it.

I Believe: ADHD is not a mental illness even though the government says it is. It is an amazing blessing if you learn how to use it and stop using it to play a victim. Depression is significantly more serious, and everyone should be taught to recognize warning signs in school so that we are better prepared as a society, to help those who need us in the future.

Live Without: Passion isn't everything, but everything is better with passion, especially if you have ADHD. I hope that you all find that passion about something or someone. Never stop looking for it. Once you find it, fight for it with every breath. And guys, here is something I used to do when I wanted some romance in my life, without being able to get any romance. I would go to a mall and buy a couple dozen long stem roses with individual water picks on each. Then I would randomly hand a rose to women I passed walking around the mall or on the way back to my hotel. It always made me remember Kandal.

Fairy Tale: Follow your heart. As much as I would have loved to have given my life to Tina, and as much as she was wonderful and deserving of better than me; by following my heart and waiting for my ex-wife, I have been blessed by the most wonderful life I could have ever imagined.

Captivate: Finding someone who captivates you like this will help you to open up so you can captivate others. Do not link this solely to physical beauty. It might just as easily be someone's laugh, their confidence, or a voice on the telephone.

Stranger: Keep your heart open and always encourage creative imagination in kids. They will likely grow up soon enough and become mindless drones. Do not be a catalyst to this loss of innocence.

Sands of Society: There is always a silver lining. Find it.

Feeling Underdressed: May we find a way to give fresh starts to those who need them before we lose our opportunity, and our chance to be the best of what makes us human.

Could I?: Anything worth having is worth working for and waiting for.

Young Love: Take a personality test (or two) because this will give you huge insights into who you are and why you do the things you do. Live your life without thinking you have to change who you are to please someone else... and find someone who will put up with your faults because you make it worth the effort for them. Don't forget to make it worth the effort.

The Bridge: Suicide is a dark and horrible thought that has hit very close to my life, but if we don't talk about it, we learn nothing; and if we learn nothing, then the greatest loss in suicide is to the living.

Amanda: As hard as it is to say, the only lesson I have is to avoid long distance romance if possible. Find a better job at home or move your family. Long distance love can work but the effort is immense, as is the risk. This is coming from a man who has done it more than once and will do it again in the future. It is a part of the life I chose.

The Puzzle: Use empathy and compassion accordingly. People dealing with loss of a loved one may need your support. Probably not me, but most other people. I say probably because I cannot imagine losing my wife or any of my kids. I might need your support after all.

Fear not Fear: How we overcome our fears helps us to learn and grow so we can better handle future fears. These lessons reinforce the idea that fear can be a positive quality.

Storms: Know your flaws and respect the people who put up with them... especially when thinking of their flaws. Invest time thinking of how your strengths can help you overcome the flaws in others before they bring out flaws in your personality. For the record, 24 years later, I still love storms and spend way too much time in them to be healthy.

The Knight: More of an instruction, but if you have some free time, donate it to a youth organization so that you can be an example of a great role model. If you do not have the free time, make it. If you are not a great role model, find one to learn from. Our future generations need you very much. We need to teach our children to want more and to expect more, of themselves, and others. Men need to know there is more to being a man, than just being a male, and women need to know that they do not have to accept anything less than the knight of their dreams.

Education: There is no such thing as quality time without quantity time. The idea that you could spend one hour a night with your children and have the same effect on them as a stay at home parent spending 12-16 hours a day with them is pure nonsense. The same logic works for your marriage.

Tragic Loss: If you are making bad life choices, you probably should not try to resolve those situations with more bad life choices. I am not a huge fan of seeking help from mental health professionals because I am as stubborn as they come, but I am a strong advocate of help for those who need it (many mental health professionals are already making notes to look me up later).

If you keep finding yourself in a deeper hole, no matter what you try to do to improve your life, you need to do two things. First, stop digging. Clearly the same level of thinking that put you in the hole cannot help you escape. Secondly, seek out help from a friend who has what you want, a mentor with a vested interest in your future, or a professional who understands what you are going through.

Muse: Believe in yourself. You don't need me or some actor, musician, or anyone else to convince you. It starts with you choosing to believe that you can do anything you want... even write a haiku.

From Misery to Happiness

DON'T FORGET TO SIGN UP FOR OUR NEWSLETTER

For special offers (all e-books go on sale for 99 cents with every new book release), giveaways, discounts, bonus content, updates from the authors and publisher, info on new releases, and other great reading...

www.KawaliPublishing.com

Special Thanks

I would like to thank the following amazing people for supporting my love of poetry through the Internet while I was divorced...

CANADA

Jennifer Prior, Shaun Dmytrowich, Peggy Toms, Andrew Toms, Jennifer Shaw, Sharon Kedra, Teri Hammel, Ken & Donna Demster, Justyne Kawalilak, Marcel Jean, Tim & Tania Blokland, Chuck Lott, Sharalee & George, Paul Keene, Leta Beal, Tina & Ryanne, Ryan & Eva, Dena Arsenault, Lisa & Austin Reed, Ken & Denise Holman, Gerry McGuire, Shelley Moroz, Russell Yorke, and Jan & Deb from Stoney Creek.

USA

Dena Griffith, Diana Nelson, Kandie Walker, Trevelyn Palmore, Leslie Bennett, Robin Alexandra, Lou Hertz, Judy Littrell, Lisa Hefner, Melanie Bolton, Jodi Digraziano, Victoria from Orange CA, Julie Carter, Barbara Werth, Kelley Haymen, Toni Petrillo, Deborah Poling, Dale Duncan, Naomi Cuevas, Michael Dorado, and J. Copeland from Austin.

INTERNATIONAL

Daniella Pace (Switzerland), Sandra Henry (Australia), Michelle Amess (Australia), Shadi Sarhan (Amman-Jordan), Michelle Yap (Malaysia), Sonia (South Africa), Carolyn Crawford (Australia), Cheryl & John White (Australia), Charlene Robbins (Guam), Keryn Valentine (New Zealand), Gaelle Dupre (France), Aksel Lian (Norway), Tino Jokisch (Germany), and Zarla Gibson (Australia).

These people can't understand how much their support 25 years ago meant to me. Thank you for all the postcards.

...and I love you if you searched for Steph Waloon and you love her as much as I do. Hopefully she keeps making YouTube videos, reading 50 books a year, and posting amazing reviews. She is wonderfully inspiring and has such a bright future.

Acknowledgements

This book would not have been published without the help of my family, and they need a mention due to their unbelievable support. Chelsey and Dion, Chantell and Matt, Ryan and Helen, Raimond, and Randal; thank you sincerely. Remy and Russel were there for moral support.

Kickstarter Acknowledgement Section

I wanted a special section to acknowledge those awesome individuals who supported us generously during our Kickstarter campaign. These people believed in my poetry book and put up their cash in this crazy world of unknowns, and I want you to know them by more than just name.

Arioch Morningstar

"Superbacker" Arioch, backed my book, along with 332 other Kickstarter campaigns. His first campaign was a Mur Lafferty book over nine years ago and his favorite Kickstarter purchase was a Lords of Acid album in 2017. Arioch shares his life online and holds nothing back. I can't imagine someone this open has too many secrets, but by the time he finishes this book he will know that he is not alone.

Arioch needs to be commended for the fact that he had supported less than ten campaigns before a pandemic took such a toll on so many. He has since proceeded to support hundreds of creative individuals in the past few months alone.

Lara Abulawi

From Misery to Happiness was the 753rd Kickstarter project that Lara backed. There is an excellent article about "Superbacker" Lara on blog.backerclub.co where she confesses to investing in nearly 1000 campaigns between crowdfunding sources.

Growing up in Mozambique and Portugal, I am sure that she could write a few books on her childhood. If you asked Lara to tell you something interesting about herself, she might say (she actually did)… "I feel too much, I have a weird empathy with anyone near me. I have a photographic memory and because of that, is hard to forgive people because I never forget. But mainly I feel too much."

To never forget can be both a blessing and a curse. And feelings can be kind of annoying as well.

A special thanks to Cydnee, my 9-year-old who wanted her name in print so badly that she was willing to lay in bed and listen to me read poetry until she fell asleep more than once. Her siblings consider this child abuse.

Reading Suggestions

Hopefully there will be more poetry books published by Shayne in the very near future.

Currently you can pre-order his first Children's book…

Princess Sparkle Makes a Friend.

Purchase other books to fall in love with directly from Shayne at www.KawaliPublishing.com or any online retailer.

You can also ask your library to bring in our books as well.

About the Author

Shayne is a writer, mostly. He is currently happily married to his ex-wife and they reside in St. Albert, Alberta, Canada, where they raised most of their nine children. He has been a professional geek for over two decades and has been an independent consultant for half of that time. He tries to divide his days evenly between his four passions; working with technology, writing anything and everything, spending as much time as humanly possible with his family, and volunteering for several organizations that benefit youth.

He has been published in several magazines and online publications. He loves speaking to crowds of any size and shares his life online.

If any of these things can be done from a motorhome or a hammock, that is where you will find Shayne.

Website:	www.KawaliPublishing.com
Facebook:	@KawaliPublishing
Instagram:	@KawaliPublishing
Twitter:	@KawaliPublish

In order to have text on the spine,

Amazon requires that I not whine…

About taking another look,

and adding 20 pages to the book.

Extra page one.

Extra page two.

Extra page three.

Extra page four.

Do I need periods if they aren't complete sentences?

Extra page five

Extra page six

Extra page seven.

I think I like it better with the period.

Extra page eight.

Extra page nine.

Extra page ten.

Extra page 11.

The rules change with every generation. I was taught any number 12 or larger should be written out, but not eleven.

Extra page 12.

But now they teach that any number ten or larger should be written out. I am unsure of what changed in the universe that made this change so important that it needed to happen.

Extra page 13.

Extra page 14.

Extra page 15.

Actually, we are not going to need an extra 20 pages.

Extra page 16.

This is the 98th page of the book including all the front matter.

Extra page 17.

And we only need to hit 100 pages so that we will be able to put text on the spine of the book.

Extra pages 18.

This is page 100 for Amazon. Now they should be okay with changing the cover.

And the last few pages resemble modern poetry books more than the first 82 pages do.

Thank you for your patience with this.

Extra page 19.

I came so close to 20

Wait... I did not number the first page where I explained that Amazon required 20 extra pages. Which means I did actually add 20 pages.

Until now.

Now I have added 21.

I love that you read this far. We have a lot in common.

Unless you were annoyed by this.

If you are saddened that there are actually no more pages,

please go to **www.KawaliPublishing.com**

and subscribe to our newsletter or just look around at our family.

www.ingramcontent.com/pod-product-compliance
Lightning Source LLC
Chambersburg PA
CBHW050441010526
44118CB00013B/1621